Vazquez Lozano, Gustavo A.
Javier Chichari
2013 5/16

D0101145

OFFICIAL
DISCARD

JAVIER "CHICHARITO" HERNÁNDEZ

TO THE TOP!

2011 In October, Manchester renews his contract for another five years.
Hospitalized in New Jersey for mild concussion, on July 26.
Javier wins the Top Scorer award and MVP of the CONCACAF Gold
Cup tournament.
Wins the Sir Matt Busby trophy awarded by Manchester fans to the
best club player on May 18.

2010 Announces his engagement with Manchester United, in April.
Says goodbye to Chivas during the inauguration of Omnilife stadium, on June 30. Scores the first goal in the history of the site.
Chicharito jumps to international fame with his World Cup goal
against France, on July 17.
Debuts at Manchester United and scores his first goal on July 28.

2009 Scores eleven goals for Chivas, becoming the third scorer in the
Mexican League Opening.

2008 Considers retirement after one season feeling ignored in
Guadalajara.

2007 Participates in the U-20 Cup in Canada, scoring his first goal in international competitions.

2006 Debuts in the first division in a match against Necaxa. Scores his
first goal as a professional.

1996 Joins the basic forces of Guadalajara club at the age of nine.

1988 Javier Hernandez Balcazar is born in Guadalajara, June 1.

© 2013 by Mason Crest, an imprint of National Highlights, Inc.

All rights reserved. No part of this publication may be reproduced or transmitted in any form or by any means, electronic or mechanical, including photocopying, recording, taping, or any information storage and retrieval system, without permission from the publisher.

ISBN-13: 978-1-4222-2660-5 (hc) — 978-1-4222-9201-3 (ebook)

Printing (last digit) 9 8 7 6 5 4 3 2 1
Printed and bound in the United States of America.
CPSIA Compliance Information: Batch #S2013. For further information, contact Mason Crest at 1-866-MCP-Book.

ABOUT THE AUTHORS:

Gustavo Vazquez-Lozano was born in Aguascalientes, Mexico. He is a writer and independent publisher. He is the author of *La estrella del sur* (Ediciones SM, 2003) and *Everything About the Beatles* (Otras Inquisiciones, 2010).

Federico Vargas Benard was born in Mexico City. He is regular contributor to the sports section in *La Jornada de Aguascalientes* newspaper.

Photo credits: EFE/Paul Buck: 24; EFE/Robin Parker: 18; Shutterstock: 1, 2, 4, 7, 10, 12, 14, 16, 17, 20, 23, 26, 29, 30; Wikimedia: 13.

TABLE OF CONTENTS

Javier "Chicharito" Hernandez is one of the best young players in Mexico today.

CHAPTER 1

Call of Destiny

THE TIMING COULD NOT BE MORE APPROPRIATE. On June 17, 2010, for its second match in the World Cup in South Africa, the Mexican team was in desperate need of a hero. After a draw against the host team in the tournament opener, achieving a victory was now a matter of life and death.

A defeat would amount to another four years of waiting time for the Mexican team. The challenge was not easy. The Green Team was going to play against the powerful French, who had always defeated the Mexicans in the history of FIFA World Cups. Despite the distance from their home country, the Mexicans did not lack motivation. They had jumped into the lawn of Peter Mokaba stadium to find painted green supporters, the representative color of their supporters; the Mexican national anthem was echoed throughout the stadium. At the start of the action, France led violent attacks toward the goal line and, despite some flashes of the national team, Mexico had to go to the halftime without scoring.

Well into the second half, Coach Javier Aguirre of Mexico decided to take risks and give a chance to Javier Hernandez, a.k.a. Chicharito, a 22-year-old relative newcomer, who was warming up on the bench. Some viewed him as the hope of that World Cup. At 17 minutes of the second half, the young man dribbled with amazing speed towards the French goal line for a showdown with goalkeeper Hugo Lloris. A quick movement and the ball was inside the net. Throughout the stadium and across the world, particularly in the city of Guadalajara, the ground itself seemed to vibrate in what was to become a victory for the Mexicans. Javier "Chicharito" Hernandez, had just scored the critical goal not only for the match, but for his soccer career.

Good Fortune

The most fascinating thing about that goal, as if it was a decree of fate, was that 56 years earlier the player's grandfather, Tomas Balcazar, had also scored a goal for Mexico under the same circumstances: during a World Cup, in a match against France, and at the age of 22. From that cold South African night, the name Javier Hernandez, which had remained exclusively inside soccer circles, pierced through the boundaries of sports to become a national obsession.

Who was this baby-faced boy scout who had concentrated the hopes and joy of an entire country in his figure? Where had he come from and how had he come to that moment of celebrity that every footballer craves?

Like Father, like Son

Javier Hernandez Balcazar saw the first light of day in the city of Guadalajara, Jalisco, Mexico, on June 1, 1988, in a family that was destined to produce good athletes. His father's name is Javier Hernandez Gutierrez and he once played for Tecos of Guadalajara; he was also part of the national team that competed in the FIFA World Cup in Mexico, 1986. Short sized and green eyed, his physical appear-

ance earned him the nickname of "Pea." The Pea was known for his ability to score with both feet. He used to take his son Javier to the Abraham Lincoln school in Guadalajara, where he enrolled at the age of six. The Pea took him by the hand and into the classroom and as he entered the school, many children—and some of their parents—approached him for autographs.

Until his father retired as a player, young Javier liked to accompany him to the stadium to watch him play and enjoy the company of other professional players. It seemed only natural that the Pea's friends and stadium staff began calling him "Chicharito," or "little pea." Since childhood, the boy showed a very definite interest in soccer. Many remember him chatting with players in the dressing room and studying his dad's game from the bench, with a look of admiration in his face.

Chicharito was studying English very hard, a skill that would be very helpful later on. "He then had a very strict English teacher," recalls Sara Carrillo, his first teacher. "But unlike other children, he never had problems with her. He showed a great interest in sports. Above all, he was a very happy kid."

Despite his young age, the big boys of the school wanted Javier playing with them.

> Javier comes from a family of players who were part of México's national team in two FIFA World Cups: 1954 and 1986.

Guadalajara is Mexico's second largest city. Javier decided to pick a favorite band, actress, and drink at an early age. He was preparing for future interviews he would do when he became famous.

To see him play was a spectacle.

Basic Forces Guadalajara

Javier's career began in the basic forces, or lower division, of Guadalajara, which he joined at age nine. Guadalajara is one of the most popular teams in the country and has one of the largest number of supporters, if not the largest. Chivas has won the Mexican league more times than any team and its unique feature is that it will hire only Mexican born players, a policy that has earned the club the affection of many in the country.

For Javier, those early years were marked by hard work and sweat. He dreamed of joining Chivas's first division team, or Holy Flock, as this red-stripped team is also known. Chicharito showed a love for learning and hardly missed a class. Many times, when the session was over and the rest of the boys went home, he stayed to practice.

"Since the beginning he showed an interest to become a leader," says Gabriel Lopez, his first coach. "He trained and exercised in things that other children didn't care about. He practiced shooting with both feet and was disciplined. It was like deep inside he knew that he had soccer in his blood and he could not waste any time." However, in the beginning this dedication was not always rewarding in the way he wanted, in spite of doing things right.

First Disappointment

Nothing is easy in the life of a young star. The road to success is full of setbacks and apparent failures. No one understands this better than Javier Hernandez—an impatient achiever. Eager to taste the glory, he soon learned that serenity and perseverance would also be part of his initiation as an athlete.

It was the year 2005 and at 16 he was part of Chivas Coras, a subsidiary of

Chivas Guadalajara, where he started to rise to prominence for his good play. That year Mexico formed a youth team to compete in the FIFA U-17 World Cup, in Peru. The boys had a clear mission in their minds: to return to Mexico as world champions. That team had promising players, like Giovanni Dos Santos, Carlos Vela, Efrain Juarez, Pablo Barrera and Hector Moreno, led by Coach Jesus Ramirez. Mexico arrived in Lima as a serious contender. A month later, before 40,000 spectators, they would repay such confidence, lifting the cup at the Estadio Nacional in Lima, Peru.

It was a historic moment for the country, since it was the first championship for Mexico in that category, but a very sad one for Javier, who had not been summoned and had fallen in an impasse. But he had a guardian angel, Jorge Vergara, the Chivas president, who upon learning of Chicharito´s low spirits, had decided to give him a present that he would never forget: paid travel expenses for him and his family to attend the final match of the U-17 World Cup, where Mexico beat Brazil three goals to zero.

Javier remembers that moment with a mixture of sadness and appreciation: "In Peru, everything was very complicated . . . Jorge Vergara took us, my friend Chore and I and our families, to watch the final of the U-17 World Cup. . . . My grandparents went too. . . . When we were in the stadium . . . I felt that I was not part of what was

happening . . . something which was such a beautiful moment for my country."

Javier, who throughout his career has shown great modesty and work ethic, was determined to carry on and not to pay much attention. Much of that attitude comes from his grandmother. They were witnessing the youth team's moment of triumph when, in his own words: "My grandmother gets close to me, I'm in tears and enjoying it all and she says, 'Son, don't worry, it was not your turn, today was not your time, but your time will come.'" These words made a strong impression on Javier, who upon seeing his companions crowned as champions, decided to work harder. As the boy's grandmother supposed, Chicharito's story of success was just beginning. From that moment, it would explode dramatically.

> At the start of his time in Chivas's basic forces, the celebrity of Javier's dad and grandfather was more hindrance than help to his career. Some said that he was being considered only for being the son of the Pea, star of the Mexican team in 1986. It was only through perseverance and professionalism that Chicharito could earn a name for himself as a player.

CHAPTER 2

Fall and Rise

THE OPPONENT WAS THE LIGHTNINGS OF NECAXA, and Javier Hernandez was destined to experience one of the most memorable nights of his career. At 18, he was finally making his debut in the first division of professional soccer with Chivas of Guadalajara. The setting was at the Jalisco stadium.

The match was 3-0 in favor of Chivas. In the second half, Javier entered the field ready for his first appointment with professional soccer. A few minutes later, almost at the end of the game, he received the ball inside the goal area. With impressive composure, he charged and scored. That appeared to be the first professional goal of Javier and his entry into the history of Mexican soccer. "Welcome, Chicharito," an euphoric voice was heard over the TV transmission, "to Mexican soccer!"

"It was the perfect debut," said the Chivas striker afterward. "It was the first time I was called to play, the first time I was on the bench, the first time I played (in the first division), and the first time I scored."

However, that spectacular goal would be the only one Chicharito would score in eight games between 2006 and 2007. Javier would play for Guadalajara again in 2007 and 2008, but would not to be able to score.

International Competition

Two years after the 2007 World Cup in Peru, it was time for Mexico to participate again in another World Youth Cup, this time the FIFA U-20 Cup in Canada, with a big difference: Chicharito was invited and he had two more years of experience and growth.

Chivas of Guadalajara is the most successful first division club in Mexico. They have won 11 titles. It is the only club in Mexico to play without foreigners. Chivas was the top club in the amateur era of Mexican soccer also, with 13 titles.

Over a hundred teams had fought for a place in the qualifying rounds. Mexico won its ticket and Javier was eager to demonstrate his capabilities. Finally, the long hours of work were going to bear fruit.

In Canada, he played five games as a substitute and, when the team played against Gambia, he scored his first international goal. Mexico fell short to reach the quarter-finals, as they were eliminated by Argentina, who in the end would be crowned as champions. A somewhat bittersweet experience for young Chicharito, certainly not as bitter as in 2005, when he had seen the glory of Mexico from the crowd, but also sweet for having had the chance to play against great teams. In the end, the general feeling was that they could have done more.

Over the edge

On returning from the World Youth Cup, anyone would have believed that the opportunities were open for Javier. However, things seemed, ironically, going in reverse. Chicharito had earned his place in the first team of Chivas, but the mere fact of having a membership was not enough. During his first three years with the team, between 2006 and 2008, he played 36 times, most of them as a substitute and scored only five goals, one in seven games on average. The worst was that he we being considered less and less and, in fact, he was being kept on the bench as a reserve. Meanwhile, other players, younger newcomers, enjoyed the coach's preferences. Javier began to despair. Feeling unappreciated, he seriously considered retirement. It was the biggest crisis of his career.

"There was so much on my mind in those years . . . I doubted if I could really

Soccer video games are one of Javier's biggest hobbies. Javier used to say that his counterpart on the screen was better than the real one, since the virtual one was already playing in Europe.

Chicharito once almost retired from soccer. Despite having a membership in Chivas of Guadalajara, his participation in the early years was low and other young players received more attention. Javier began to doubt whether he could play soccer, even though people told him he was doing fine. It was only through determination to succeed and the support of his family that Mexico did not lose this great player.

play soccer and if it was . . . the road that God wanted for me. It was hard to see the list of players every week and not being there and . . . being kept on the bench. . . . Suddenly, I was no longer enjoying my profession."

The momentary lack of confidence and poor performance, a must in every athlete's career, seemed like an insurmountable obstacle in the mind of this 20 year old man, who was skilled, with great promise, but very worried. Fortunately, as in other times in his life, he had the support of his family. "One night I was there with my family, talking . . . and I realized that . . . I had to enjoy not just the weekends, but every Monday, every Tuesday, every practice, the esteem of my classmates. I was in the best team in Mexico . . . I was healthy, I had my family, which are very important things."

Chivas of Guadalajara

After a painful season, both emotionally and physically, where dark clouds seemed to hover over Chicharito, good times finally arrived. The 2009 Aperture was the occasion for Javier to become a sports figure. That season would be the first truly rewarding experience of his career. In 17 games he scored eleven goals and became the third top scorer in the tournament. He earned the definite membership and better yet, without knowing it, he was being watched attentively by European scouts.

His style was cheerful and he had a winning attitude, he had a great scoring instinct and showed obvious enthusiasm when he was on the lawn. Above all, he was fearless, which is perhaps the more appreciated trait in soccer. And that was not all. Javier Hernandez kept his "good boy" image and behavior: while playing for Guadalajara, he kept studying business administration in college and lived with his parents; he showed great discipline in practices and, despite his growing celebrity, he was discreet and exhibited a spirit of fellowship both to their peers and fans.

The 2010 Bicentennial tournament, named so as to celebrate two centuries of independence in Mexico, was the reaffirmation of what everybody already knew: Javier had come to accomplish great things. He scored six goals in the first three games of the tournament, helping Guadalajara to achieve its best start in the short tournament in history, with eight consecutive victories.

The Secret Negotiations

Chicharito was Chivas's new sensation. He

Chicharito celebrates a goal for Chivas in 2010.

was on a scoring spree, a natural-born forward, which is scarce in Mexican soccer. Historically, Mexican teams play a good game, but score few goals. It was then that Manchester United of England, considered one of the best clubs in the world, decided to roll the dice and make him an offer.

During February and March 2010 Manchester's chief scout, Jim Lawlor, had visited Mexico to see Javier play. When he was convinced that he had a true sporting promise before his eyes, Lawlor sent an encouraging report to England recommending his hiring.

The negotiation was handled in much secrecy. The media did not know anything about it. To divert attention, in the sixth day of the tournament Javier was announced to have suffered a thigh injury. Nobody ever said how serious the injury was, so no one paid much attention. His teammates did not suspect anything either. Not even his grandfather, Tomas Balcazar, always close to his grandson to encourage him with advice, knew the truth.

On the morning of April 8, 2010, with evident joy, Javier Hernandez announced his engagement with Manchester United from Old Trafford stadium, also known as the Theatre of Dreams. The purchase had been completed for an undisclosed amount, which was apparently the highest figure ever paid for a Mexican player. While the work permit by the British government was pending—it would be granted on May 27—at that time there was only room for happiness and joy for his supporters.

Chivas Top Scorer

Certainly the news of Chicharito's transfer took Mexican fans by surprise, due in part to the speed with which everything had happened. Chicharito had not played the last five games with Chivas, not even the classic match against Club America. The fans were awaiting the return of their striker and instead they got a surprise announcement that, Chicharito was leaving for England.

Javier negotiated his contract with Manchester in absolute secrecy. Not even his grandfather, always close to him, knew of the trip to England. Don Thomas thought that his grandson was on a flight to Atlanta to enjoy a vacation.

Javier returned to Mexico to finish the tournament with Chivas. But from the next summer, the Tapatio idol would change the red stripes uniform for another red outfit, that of the Devils of Manchester United. Ending on a high note, Javier finished the Bicentennial tournament as the top scorer and was awarded the distinction as Best Striker.

His future was now laid out: the Red Devils expected the arrival of Chicharito on July 1st. But before leaving for Europe, Javier Hernandez had another dream pending, the most important in the life of any soccer player: to play for the national team in the World Cup, which would take place in South Africa. The stars were beginning to align for him.

Chicharito prepares for the winning goal against Valencia, one of the best teams in the league, during a match in September 2010.

CHAPTER 3

The Little Pea Ripens

LIFE IN MEXICO BECOMES PARALYZED WHENEVER THE NATIONAL team plays in the World Cup. A game by the Green Team is one of the few events capable of bringing men and women, big and old, in front of the TV, including those who are not interested in soccer. The World Cup is almost a religion.

Mexico has had a long tradition in World Cup tournaments. Its first participation dates back to 1930. When the team can't get a ticket to the World Cup, it's practically a national tragedy.

The Decisive Cup

In 2010, the Mexicans had succeeded in the qualifiers and their participation was assured. The goals that Javier had scored in training matches against Bolivia, New Zealand, North Korea, and the spectacular goal against the mighty Netherlands, had earned him a place in coach Aguirre's team.

Mexico was in one of the most difficult groups, with France, Uruguay and the host South Africa. Bets were against the tricolored team. Mexico's first game in the World Cup was not easy, facing the host team at the inaugural match. It was a rough game with a lot of kicks, Mexico was at a disadvantage and had to paddle against the current. Javier joined in the second half and at minute 33 of the game he saw his teammate Rafael Marquez score to help Mexico earn a draw. Chicharito did not score in that match, but there were still two games to try.

The Providential Goal

For the second match against France, the Mexican players were focused and

15

more prepared. They did not speak with the media. Speculation was huge. The coach unveiled his lineup for that cold night. Chicharito again started on the bench.

The Mexican team had possession of the ball and began to devise what would be one of the most memorable games in Mexican soccer history. Giovanni Dos Santos almost had the first goal but missed. The crowd of supporters gasped. When the second half started, it seemed like there was something missing—an agitator, a

At the end of the 2010 World Cup Javier Hernandez was recognized as the fastest player in the competition, reaching speeds of more than 19 miles per hour.

spark, a movement, whatever. At minute 55 Javier Hernandez finally entered the lawn. At minute 63 he ran into the goal area. Rafael Marquez, the team captain, sent a cross pass where Javier stood alone against the goalkeeper.

Fans from all over Mexico held their breath, and the television commentator begged: "Do not fail, do not fail." It was not necessary, because Javier was hungry to score. The Mexican fans in the stadium jumped from their seats. Chicharito ran into the goal area alone, faced the goal-keeper, easily eluded him with a break to the left, and scored for Mexico.

The match ended 2-0 in favor of Mexico. That providential goal would be a turning point in Javier's career.

Mexican honor

With the win against France in its pocket, the Mexican national team took a huge step towards the second round of the South Africa World Cup, a round that always has been a headache. Mexico had to face Argentina. Before the game against the White and Sky Blue, there was much talk about Javier: whether or not to have him, if he was real or a fantasy, if it should be he who had the leadership. When the game started, speculation ended. Javier was in and he scored the goal of honor in a widely criticized game, both because of the refer-ees' decisions—Argentina scored in offside position—and a poor national performance that included defender Ricardo Osorio's goal against his own team.

Mexico has never been able to play a fifth game in a World Cup. Javier Hernandez's goal against Argentina, if it had come earlier, might have changed history.

This ended Mexico's participation in the World Cup, again, with a bittersweet taste. Fortunately for Javier, he won the award as the fastest player of the tournament: 19.8 miles per hour. And the sweetest was still to come.

Manchester United

After the World Cup, Javier boarded a plane to the United Kingdom, where he joined the ranks of Manchester United for spring training. Manchester United, also known as the Red Devils, is one of the most popular and successful teams in the world, not only in soccer but in many sports. It has millions of followers worldwide. Among its past glories, they were the first team to win the European Cup, in 1968. The club has also won the Premier League title 19 times. Unforgettable players like Bobby Charlton, David Beckham, and Cristiano Ronaldo have shone in its ranks. Sir Alex Ferguson, the club's current manager, is considered the most successful coach in English soccer history.

The mission was considerable and pressure was also an unavoidable factor. Some said that the Mexican player would have no place on the English club—not for lack of talent, but because Manchester was already a very good team. Javier would play side-by-side with world-class players like Wayne Rooney, Rio Ferdinand, Paul Scholes, Ryan Giggs, Antonio Valencia, and Luis Nani. Competition inside the club itself was huge and many wondered if Chicharito would get playing time.

Several days of speculation passed before Javier could answer those doubts on the lawn. On July 28 Chicharito had the chance, when he played the first preseason game for United. The club was going to play against a team from stars from Major League Soccer, a professional league in the United States.

Sir Alex Ferguson is the longest serving manager of an European soccer club. He began his career with Manchester in 1986. In 2011 he celebrated his 25 years at the club. Since his arrival, Manchester has become England's ultimate champion and has twice won the Champions League.

Chicharito celebrates scoring a goal for Manchester United.

Sixteen minutes into the second half, Sir Alex Ferguson called Chicharito to go into the game. The crowd at the stadium stood up to greet him. The hearts of hundreds or perhaps thousands of Mexicans in the stadium and millions on television throbbed at top speed. Javier was jumping near the line of the field to release anxiety and then trotted onto the lawn. Now was his chance to prove that the English club's confidence was justified.

From the moment he came into the game Chicharito was active. He made good passes and tried to attack the goal. But Manchester had not hired him for that,

they wanted him to score. As the soccer saying goes: the striker lives and dies for the sake of the goal.

"The Little Pea Is Here"

At minute 84, Javier escaped from his defenders and was left alone near the goal area. Darren Fletcher noticed this movement and made a great pass that left Javier in good position. The Stars' goalkeeper was desperate trying to shrink the space between them. Javier saw him coming and still away from the target he pumped his shot over the goalkeeper's body. It was a risky move, worthy of a gambler. The ball was buried in the net. Javier had scored his first goal for Manchester.

The crowd was euphoric and Hernandez celebrated with his teammates, who hugged him and patted on his head. That was not an ordinary goal; it was his first goal and his greeting to the new home. The television camera captured the coach, who was smiling and clapping for his new pupil. That was the Mexican's first spark in the English club, and certainly not the last.

Fighting on two fronts

One of the terms of the contract with Manchester stated that Chicharito would have the opportunity to play one last game for Guadalajara to say goodbye to his Mexican fans in a friendly match against none other than Manchester. Symbolically,

Javier played the first half for Guadalajara and the second with the Red Devils.

The match took place on June 30 on a hot Mexican afternoon. Javier started with Chivas and had the honor of scoring the first long distance, spectacular goal in the history of the Omni life stadium. It was the ultimate gift for the team where he had come from. Always careful not to hurt anyone's feelings, the young clasped hands apologizing to his future colleagues, but also thanking the fans that had packed the 45,000-seat stadium.

Thus Javier Hernandez said goodbye to the crowd of supporters in Guadalajara, scoring the first goal, apologizing in the celebration and making his fans happy. Days later, nearly 9,000 miles away, he would make his historic debut for Manchester United.

> **During his first season with Manchester, Javier scored important goals for the team. He scored the winning goal against Valencia in the Champions League; he scored the goal that allowed Manchester to move to the next round of the Carling Cup against Wolverhampton; he also scored the fastest goal of the season, in the 35th second of the game against Chelsea. He scored the winning goal against Everton for a record 13 consecutive victories at Old Trafford, and again scored the first goal against Chelsea in the Champions League. Of the many goals that Javier scored, a lot were of immense importance to his club.**

Chicharito pursues the ball in a match against Chile in 2011.

CHAPTER 4

A Fantastic Year

JAVIER SCORED HIS FIRST OFFICIAL GOAL FOR MANCHESTER United in the Community Shield match, the first of a total of twenty that he would achieve in the inaugural season. In this manner he would equal the record set by Luis Garcia who had the highest number of goals scored by a Mexican player in his debuting season in Europe.

For its circus-like quality, Chicharito's first goal against Chelsea traveled all around the world: Antonio Valencia made a cross pass to the goal area and Javier hit the ball twice, first with his foot and then with his face, all in a matter of seconds. It was without doubt one of the funniest goals of the season. For Javier, it was his debut in official competitions, and also a kind of symbolic medal: his team won the title that joins the Premier and the FA Cup. Thus began the English season: one game, one goal, one title.

Adapting to A New Life

Chicharito's first few months in England would be dreamy. "Some days I wake up and I just can't believe it," he said. "I'm living in this great country, playing for the best club in the world and in the best league in the world." His family had also moved there to support him and provide company. His routine was simple and well planned. He got up at eight o'clock, had breakfast and went to practice. He liked to arrive early and work overtime, like in his years in Chivas. After training, he ate with the family. They ordered ingredients online for Grandma and Mom to cook Mexican dishes for Chicharito, but they also experimented with the local flavor.

Upon arrival at Manchester, Javier thought that he would be in the reserves and would play only a few minutes with the main team.

Like many foreigners, one of the most difficult adjustments was learning to drive with the wheel on the right side, as you drive in England. "It's like they turned everything upside down," he said a few weeks after his arrival, "you just . . . have to practice a lot and there it is. It then seems normal and you begin to drive better."

Professionally, the situation couldn't be better. Manchester was first and Javier was playing frequently. He rewarded his manager with beautiful and much celebrated goals.

Dream Season

The period running from October 2010 to March 2011 would represent the highest point so far; he was awarded Player of the Month trophy in the Premier League three times: November, January, and April. Javier stood out among 500 players in England and began to attract stares and comments from all over Europe, thanks to the forcefulness and visual quality of his moves.

On October 24th, within that scoring streak, he achieved what no other Mexican had done. Manchester United visited Stoke City in a league match. Javier scored one of the best goals of the season and the winning goal in the final minutes, becoming the first Mexican ever to score two goals in a Premier League match.

Speaking of spectacular, Chicharito scored the first goal with the back of his head, his back to the crossbar. A center sent by Nemanja Vidic gave Javier a clear scoring opportunity. The only problem was that he had his back to the goal. The young man rose in the air like driven by a spring and he hit the ball—with the back of his head! The ball was with him, it took direction and ended up in the net, thus scoring one of the most difficult goals of the year.

The rest of the season continued with frenetic pace and Javier took advantage of it, scoring the fastest goal of the season, only 35 seconds after the start of the game against Chelsea.

End of the Season

At the end of the 2011 season Javier had become a hero for Manchester. Local newspapers and the club itself compared him with a historic player, the Norwegian Ole Gunnar Solskjaer, whom the coach used to call when the team was in trouble.

The first season in Europe ended up being one of the best for any Mexican in history. Javier was the champion of the Community Shield in his first game, he

The nickname "Chicharito" is difficult to pronounce for many English fans, so Javier was baptized as "Chico," and that has already been the theme of a song.

won individual awards along the campaign and also won the league with his club; he played the final of the Champions League with Manchester, but unfortunately they lost against Barcelona's perfect team. Finally, he won the Sir Matt Busby Player of the Year award and finished third in the competition for best young player in the English season.

With all these individual and collective distinctions, the hopes in his return to the Mexican national team were gigantic. The three-colored team, the Mexican Tricolor, would participate in the CONCACAF Gold Cup in the U.S., which would allow the winner the chance to compete in the 2013 Confederations Cup in Brazil.

2011 Gold Cup

The cup was a resounding success for Chicharito and Mexico. The team won every game they played and claimed the title after beating the tenacious American team in the final. Chicharito scored seven goals and was awarded the tournament's Golden Boot and was also named the most valuable player.

In the opening match against El Salvador, he scored the first hat-trick of his career. Against Cuba he kept his scoring spree with two goals in a match that ended 5-0. In the quarterfinals of which Mexico faced a strong Guatemala, in a much-interrupted game because of kicks and rough play, ultimately the hardest game so far.

In the semi-finals against Honduras, Mexico was the favorite. The game went

Mexico's hopes of winning the Gold Cup seemed to vanish when five players, including Guillermo Ochoa, were suspended on suspicion of using illegal substances.

into extra time. Again the goals of Javier Hernandez and Aldo de Nigris made the difference. So Mexico was in the final against the host team and CONCACAF rival: United States.

The Dreaded Rival

That final was one of the best matches of the tournament. Both teams exhibited vigorous styles and the competition was all-consuming for the whole 90 minutes.

Everything seemed lost for Mexico in the 23rd minute, down with a 2-0 score in a hostile stadium. What's more, in the 28th minute Carlos Salcido who was essential for the team suffered an injury that prevented him from continuing. When every-

Chicharito receives the Golden Boot for most goals in the Gold Cup after the final victory over the U.S. in 2011.

thing seemed lost, Javier received the ball in the midfield and made a strategic pass that left Pablo Barrera alone against goalkeeper Tim Howard. Barrera kicked with the outside of his right foot and decreased the gap to 2-1.

In the 36th minute, a good play by Giovanni Dos Santos on the left wing left the goal unguarded for Andrés Guardado to push the ball into the net. The match was now 2-2, and hopes were reborn for thousands of fans in the stadium and millions of TV spectators. It had been a crazy first half: four goals, two injured players and lots of good action. That final was showing signs to be a great match and would continue to be so in the second half.

The second half offered one of the greatest comebacks in the history of Mexican soccer. It was only the 4th minute of the game when Pablo Barrera who was in the goal area kicked a pass from Andrés Guardado to get a 2-3 score. It was a flag goal—for the euphoria produced among the supporters—and the penultimate nail in the American coffin.

The end was blunt. Javier fought for a ball in the opponent's corner area. Bocanegra pushed him and tried to steal the ball. Chicharito fought and got a rebound that came to Gerardo Torrado, who made a through pass and Giovanni Dos Santos took care of the rest. Gio took the ball inside the goal area, goalkeeper Howard was desperate to take the ball. Gio made one, two, three feints in the area. Again Bocanegra tried to catch the ball. Dos Santos cut to the left and hit the ball with little force. Eric Lichaj was waiting in the goal line trying to avoid the tragedy; he jumped with all he had and still saw the ball smashed into the corner. That was the best goal in the tournament, the winning goal for Mexico.

Chicharito scored his first hat trick in the 2011 Gold Cup, which was won by an unbeatable Mexican team. It happened in the match against El Salvador, which Mexico won by a final score of 5-0. Javier Hernandez also won the title as Top Scorer with seven goals, and was honored as the Most Valuable Player of the tournament. Some consider 2011 to be the best year in Mexican soccer history.

Chicharito participates in a fashion show in New York with Nani, his teammate with Manchester United, in 2011.

CHAPTER 5

Mexican Promise

AFTER THE GOLD CUP, JAVIER RETURNED to the ranks of Manchester. This time, there were storm clouds on the preseason and start of the official competition. Manchester had agreed to play again against the MLS stars, the same stage where Javier had debuted a year earlier. However, due to an injury Chicharito would not participate in the rematch.

Later, during the club's preseason tour in the United States, Javier suffered a concussion and was hospitalized in New Jersey on July 26. Chicharito was such a celebrity in his country, even Mexico's President Felipe Calderon sent his good wishes via Twitter.

Javier would be discharged the next day, but his afflictions continued. That's when the Guadalajara club doctor, Rafael Ortega, announced that the young man had a preexisting medical condition and was suffering from migraine headaches. With the disturbing news, Manchester decided not to risk its young striker. Javier missed the entire preseason and the start of the 2011-2012 season.

Back to Manchester

It was not until September 10 when he returned to the lineup to score goals. "Chico"—as some British media nicknamed him—made a huge comeback, with two goals, to contribute to the massive 5-0 win over Bolton Wanderers. On December 3 he was injured again in a league match against Aston Villa.

Despite his many injuries, Javier Hernandez proved that had an iron constitution that allowed him to return to the field quickly. Overcoming injuries, migraines and even some doubts, he played with personality in the 2-0 win against Queens Park. No wonder, professionalism and respect for the profession are among Javier's distinctive marks. By the beginning of 2012, Javier had returned to competition in Europe.

Chicharomania

Mexico has always suffered a "goal drought" and a lack of good forwards. So Chicharito is seen like a national treasure. Not only sports papers and programs follow his progress. Many are optimistic about a success story like his, sorely needed in a country burdened with problems. "He's the only thing Mexicans believe in right now," said writer Guadalupe Loaeza. "We do not believe in the government, or institutions or political parties. But through months and months of this crisis, Chicharito has brought us good news in front of the whole world."

"It's difficult to overemphasize what Chicharito has achieved this year and what it means to Mexicans," wrote Tom Marshall, a sportscaster in the city of Guadalajara. "There was even a debate on a radio show about whether Chicharito or the Pope had been better for the Catholic Church over the last year!" Several large

Despite his celebrity, Javier Hernandez has a cordial and friendly attitude to the fans and media, a rarity among sports celebrities.

corporations seem to be in competition to see who makes the best TV commercial with the athlete.

His fame and recognition go beyond the borders of Mexico. In Manchester, supporters sing "Chico is the man," a salsa song based on a song by José Feliciano, recorded by the World Red Army band. "The fans have been great to me. They display my name, they sing it, I am encouraged," says Javier.

The striker has continued receiving accolades in Europe. At a news conference Ferguson said that Javier was the best striker in the world in the goal area. Josep Guardiola called him a "crack" before the Champions League final. Roberto Soldado, player and captain of Valencia, admitted he wanted him in his team.

The Future

What does the future hold for Javier Hernandez? What will this young man offer to his country Mexico that loves soccer but has reached the quarterfinals at the World Cup only once? Is his destiny to become the next big soccer star, like Hugo Sanchez and Rafael Marquez, or will his star fade?

For now, the immediate future is in the ranks of Manchester United. After some weeks of speculation, in October 2011 the British team renewed his contract for another five years. Javier got a fixed salary plus incentives, depending on the team's results in different competitions. But beyond the financial rewards are the magnificent prospects under the direction of

Sir Alex Ferguson, known worldwide for what he has accomplished with other players. People like Wayne Rooney and Cristiano Ronaldo have realized their full potential under the guidance of the legendary coach.

"There is a bright future for Javier if he keeps playing like this," writes Juan Carlos Juárez, sports commentator of Tepic, Nayarit. "He's cunning, agile, he moves well, has talent and is in great shape. But the best thing for the Pea . . . is his stay at Manchester United, which is perhaps the second-best team in the world, just below Barcelona. If he can consolidate his membership, he will become one of the best strikers in the world. The winners will be the Red Devils and especially the Mexican national team, which has lacked a world-class striker."

Much will be decided in Javier's second year in Manchester. The contract's renewal doesn't necessarily mean that the player will have much playing time. It can be, in some cases, only a ploy to sell him to another club. Besides, if little was expected of the Mexican player in his first year in Europe and secondly pressure increases, especially given the good past performance. For everyone it's clear that if Javier keeps playing as he has done, developing strength and goal instinct, and above all showing such dedication, the future is bright for the now-famous player.

Chicharito in action.

Chicharito to the Max

Although Javier is now one of the best known faces in his country, he still puts value in small things in life. Recently, on receiving the title of Tourism Ambassador of the state of Jalisco, he demonstrated his worth and modesty.

"All I have are words of thanks. To the people who are here, my family, I want to apologize for not being one hundred percent a son, a brother, and nephew, a good grandson, for being a little selfish fighting for my dreams. I hope that I can be grateful. Without you I would never have accomplished anything."

At the ceremony, Javier Hernandez spoke from the heart, with tears in his eyes, referring to his family. His words reflect everything that he is: winning attitude, lack of pretension, humility; probably not the most technical player, or even the most

of effort, is perhaps the best example for young people around the world who more often think, the stories of struggle and effort do have a happy ending. Although at age 24, Chicharito is far from thinking about retirements.

His success is not due to favoritism or personal influences. It is rather a sum of effort, inspiration and self-confidence. Maybe that is why "Chico" keeps showing his eternal smile and down to earth attitude, always with a kind word for others, to show that soccer, as any good metaphor for life, is above all an expression of the struggle of the human spirit.

skilled with the ball, but surely the most charismatic dreamer that his country has ever known. Above all, this healthy and friendly Mexican, who proclaims a culture

Among Javier's many distinctions in the last two years, he was awarded the Golden Ball for Best Forward in the 2010 Bicentennial tournament; Man of the Match in the Mexico vs. France game in the World Cup; Manchester United's Player of the Month in November 2010, January and April 2011; Sir Matt Busby trophy as Player of the Year, which was voted by fans, and the Top Scorer Boot in the 2011 Gold Cup and MVP of the tournament.

FURTHER READING

Allen, Gregory. "Chicharito the great" *GQ México* (October 2011), pp. 32-40.

Bueno, José Antonio. *The History of Futbol*. Spain: Editorial Edaf, 2010.

Clavellinas, Rafael. *Training Manual and the Rules of Futbol*. Spain: Editorial Paidotribo, 2010.

EMazur, Martin. "Born to be great" *FourFourTwo Magazine* (September 2011), p. 62-65.

Torales, Guillermo. *The Language of Futbol: Dictionary of Terms and Phrases Characteristic in Mexico*. México: Editorial Trillas, 2009.

INTERNET RESOURCES

www.femexfut.org.mx

Official site of the Mexican Federation of Soccer Association AC with statistics, club profiles, youth teams and professionals, as well as the regulations of the federation.

www.chivascampeon.com

Official site of Chivas de Guadalajara, first division professional soccer team. Includes information on players, coaches, directors, statistics, scorers and facts about the club and stadium.

www.futboltotal.com.mx

One of the most comprehensive sites dedicated to soccer. In addition to information, it provides access to live games, galleries, blog and podcast.

www.espanol.manuted.com

The official website of Manchester United soccer team. Includes players biographies, history, schedules, results and information on future matches.

televisadeportes.esmas.com/futbol/

Televisa's news and features website, with videos, galleries, exclusive statistics and information about soccer and other sports. Featuring statements from several international news agencies.

INDEX